P9-EDF-158

WITHDRAWN
UTSA LIBRARIES

LEARNING TO BREATHE UNDERWATER

LEARNING TO BREATHE UNDERWATER

POEMS BY WILLIAM MEISSNER

OHIO UNIVERSITY PRESS : ATHENS, OHIO

© 1979 by William Meissner
Printed in the United States of America
All Rights Reserved

Library of Congress Cataloging in Publication Data

Meissner, William, 1948–
    Learning to breathe underwater.
    I.   Title.
PS3563.E38L4   811'.5'4   79-18881
ISBN 0-8214-0418-0
ISBN 0-8214-0426-1 pbk.

LIBRARY
The University of Texas
At San Antonio

CREDITS

I would like to thank the National Endowment for the Arts for a Creative Writing Fellowship which supported the writing of these poems.

Some of these poems were first published in the following magazines:

POETRY NORTHWEST: "The Man Who Sucked Postcards," "The Last Story of the Sightless Man's Hands," "The Phantom of the Supermarket," "The UFO in Iowa," "Death of the Track Star."

FIELD: "The Magician's Dream of Safety."

SHENANDOAH: "Deciding About Running Away to Join a Circus, Part 1," "Planting in the Back Yard."

NEW ORLEANS REVIEW: "Deciding About Running Away to Join a Circus, Part 3," "The Contortionist."

KANSAS QUARTERLY: "The Fisherman's Last Cast," "Seven A. M. Snowlot," "My Father Spoke to Me of Indians."

CHELSEA: "Returning What is Rightfully Theirs," "Message From a Found Bottle: 2"

MIDWEST QUARTERLY: "Just Passed 23, Looking for 22," "The Coal Mine Disaster's Last Trapped Man Contemplates Salvation."

PRISM INTERNATIONAL: "Journey This Night into Lightning," "About What it is Like to Die."

DECEMBER: "The Antiaircraft Hero."

DACOTAH TERRITORY: "Salvage," "Earth Man, the Harvest."

POETRY NOW: "The Widow Woman Who Hears the Bats," "Mutiny of the Animals," "The Slaughterhouse Boys."

MINNESOTA REVIEW: "Three Translations from an Old Farmer's Photograph."

NORTHEAST: "The Lines in the Road are Guesses," "The Water Tower Climbers."

CHARITON REVIEW: "Hunting for Magazines with Jerry Schultz."

THE FIDDLEHEAD: "Dance We Gave Each Other," "Deciding About Running Away to Join a Circus, Part 2," "An Airman in Europe, Listening for Echoes."

CINCINNATI POETRY REVIEW: "The Return: Song of Not Moving."

POETRY NATION: "Message From a Found Bottle: I," "Drifting, Like a Circle."

CHOWDER REVIEW: "Death of the Fisherman."

STUDIO ONE: "The Woman Who Ate Light," "Wintering in America," Where the Season of Canoes Takes Us."

GONE SOFT: "The Madman's Escape into the National Forest."

UNICORN: "Evening in a Small Town."

SOUTHERN POETRY REVIEW: "The Drowner."

CONTENTS

FOR CHRISTINE
who helped it all begin

ONE.   HOUSE OF WATER, HOUSE OF FIRE: GROWING UP NAKED

THE FATHER, WHO COULD NOT SWIM

Morning was a mouthful of water
when I first learned of dying:
Kaufman's dad was fishing when he tipped
his aluminum boat. He never heard
the shouts that flattened
on the ripples above him; he was sinking
deep into the blue waltz
of the lake
(the way my father did
when he folded the newspaper filled with wars
in half, in half
again, then pressed his creased forehead
miles into his pillow).

Somewhere a knife shreds the night
like barracuda, a bullet punctures a quiet brain
like a sliver from a nightmare:
(whatever kills another man's flesh
numbs the skin on my father's wrist).

Still brushing my teeth before school,
I heard Dad's deep breaths
behind me. I knew he wanted
to rest his leaden palm on my shoulder,
but in the bathroom mirror I watched
his wavy reflection slowly turning,
the screen door closing behind him like an eyelid.

EVENING IN A SMALL TOWN

1

The boys in undershirts smoke cigarettes in the ditch
by the railroad tracks. They know the matted grass marks
the best place to sit.

2

If I could stand, she thought,
in front of the bathroom screen,
will the lines show?
is anyone looking?

3

Pictures of naked ladies torn from magazines
do somersaults through the long weeds.
When the rain falls during the night,
their bodies will smudge into pulp.

4

Take off the rest of your nightgown
and listen to the June beetles thump
against the screen porch.
After the sun goes down, turn on
the lightbulb on the ceiling.
Will the boys that slide by on bicycles
decide to circle around the block?

5

If the train storms past,
stand closer.
Pretend,
pretend it's an earthquake.

One: The Test.
A Tightrope Walker Can Never Look Down.

The white wire cracks
a black sky 400 feet
above the parking lot,
no nets. The crowd counts
below, the back of their necks

Hardening into asphalt. He counts
his toes again and
again so he won't see
how high he is.

He would end all this, climb
down, to rest in the palm
of a hammock, like most men with glass
bones. But his feet
will not listen to him.

He imagines himself
slipping: eleven seconds
of falling   is   too   long
trying to grab
a fistful of air he knows
the uselessness of screaming

The last tight
feet, sweat finds
his eyes, his mouth
opening wide, like a
scream, or a yawn

As he thinks of the people
curled in the

Grandstand, the one
fat woman who laughs,
thinking his fall is all
part of the act.

Two:
The Only Thing a Circus Fears is Fire.

The Ringling bears shuffle close
on all hinds, their mouths
grinding on silver chains
                    two quarters buy a look
                    at the girl in the far tent
                    with the snake tattoo
                    squeezing her body (boys
                    with curling hair
                    form a stiff line)

                    25¢ to hear
                    the woman with no arms
                    play the national anthem
                    with her toes
                    "Loyal to Her Country" the sign says
The ringmaster's pockets
are cloth ears that listen for
the jingle of gold.

In the ring heat is
rising in bellies and backs
thunder thick fur
twisting outside the canvas
                    midgets pray for rain
                    fat men and the thin
                    ladies cluster

                    to the hush

of calliope

the music of smoke.

Three: Afternoon the Circus Left Town.

This could be a day without corners,
a drunken clown doing handstands on a tightrope

In a room that has stopped breathing
I almost hear music
faint as hares' footsteps,
songs I have memorized.

The wind circles in the yard, a mad dog
searching for a place to hole

the three rings are closer now

I hear my voice walking on stilts
                out the window:
        I don't care where you're going
        or how fast.

I look down at the ten roads of my fingers.

SUNDAY AFTERNOON DRIVE NEAR THE CLIFFS
OUTSIDE OF TOWN

All we kids did was ask Dad to drive off the road
a little closer to the cliff.
He cracked the ignition switch
off, let our '52 Rambler roll
gradually toward the edge
until we saw nothing but raw air
outside the windshield.
Mom squeezed his elbow
but his eyes pinched into BBs, his knuckles
clenched the wheel as though he loved
or hated it.
He eased his foot off
the wheezing brake. We rocked
nearer, gravel stuttering under tires.
He kept us there,
the dashboard clock dropping hard seconds
into the front seat,
our screams filling the back seat
like weights.
But he wouldn't
back up, as if he wanted the whole family to fly,
or die.
He laughed when he finally steered
us toward the city limits,
but all we kept seeing
were those monstrous brown boulders
far below us
looking like too many wrecked houses.

HUNTING FOR MAGAZINES WITH JERRY SCHULTZ

That Saturday morning after the rain
Schultz and I stalked the roadsides
looking for dirty magazines.
Fingernails of weeds scratched at our ankles.
We were 12, and we lived on a desert:
women were water.

We spotted a magazine spread open in the ditch—
a silky woman buzzed on the cover;
we untangled the damp grass from around it,
held it high as if it was our first caught fish.
Our eyes held their breaths.

No cars in sight, said Jerry, so we yanked
the sticking pages apart—
our stares climbed the mountains
of women's thighs,
women's bare back
ends, women's bosoms.
Then we discovered it: a page
with our first full nude.
Her arms were pale rivers
flowing out from her sides.
Our eyes spun across the page like marbles,
but her picture was too wet and blurred;
we recognized
nothing.

We held the magazine up to the
shaking sunlight, trying to trace her body
while our throbbing thumbs imagined,
imagined.

Shuffling back to Schultz's house, we
silently cursed the low clouds
that had licked our pin-up clean. We claimed
to each other how much we had seen.

Later the two of us climbed behind his barn, tried
again to push that gigantic old boulder
thundering down the hill
and into the river.

THE SCAPULAR MEDAL

Put your scapular medals around your necks, children,
the nuns told the class.
I looked at the chocolate-colored string
coiled in my palm,
tried hard not to think of nooses
and hangmen and the gallows
on that western movie when they strung up
Randolph Scott and threw his Indian friend—
boulders tied to his ankles—into the river, where
he did his last war dance on the bottom, swaying
side to side and chanting
silently.

Don Pollard flipped his scapular
over his slick hair, and Phil Kneeler made a thumbprint
before he slid his on.
We looked at each other, best buddies,
and smirked. How could we know
            that Phil would be crushed by a hoist
            ten years later in Cashman's Auto Body,
            the whole heavy car pressing
            and pressing on him
            until all the water squeezed from his forehead?
            Or that Don, who worked there too, would carry
            Phil's motionless body back and forth
            until the ambulance came?

So I looped the string over my head,
tucked it into my t-shirt, listened
as the nuns told us never take it off,
not even when swimming, because
            one day a grade school boy was swimming in a river
            and he got this terrible cramp in his chest.
            I sat at my desk, imagining the weight of his own pain
            pulling him under.
            He struggled to the surface, they said,
            one hand waving,
            one clutching the scapular.

On the bank, saved by a farmer, the boy
thanked God and Jesus
with words filled with riverwater.
So wear these to school tomorrow, the nuns said,
wear them in the future,
wear them forever.

After school I stared
at my bare chest in the mirror:
the brown string was a little road traveling
in a circle. How could I know I'd
lose it somewhere in high school?
The cool plastic picture of the saint stuck to my skin
right where my heart was.
That night I slept without winding myself in sheets.
But some nights I'd dream
            of rivers and lakes of
            trying to keep my nostrils
            above water and feeling this great weight
            crushing me down from above:
            when I tried to kick my ankles
            turned to stone and a noose strong as a wrench
            tightened around my neck.

            Those nights I'd wake up
            dripping as if I'd been deep
            underwater, and right away my damp fingers
            would rush to the square plastic island of the scapular
            and I could almost feel it buoying me,
            buoying me up.

MY FATHER SPOKE TO ME OF INDIANS

"The Blackfeet knew every grain of sand
where this farm is," he told me. "I used to hunt
arrowheads where wind
scalped the earth of grass.
I never could find one,
but you might."

I began to smell an old story on his breath,
and my ears had already run
a mile away.

"and that burial mound back in our woods—
the one shaped like a man with buck horns on his head—
they say at midnight ghosts drifted like smoke
from that mound, set fire to
the whites' houses. Settlers
hung Indian relics
above their doors for good luck."

    Next day I lay on the spine of a hill
    and told the clouds what my dad had said.
    I smiled, a tree nodded.
The night he disappeared no one
knew where. Near morning when I found him
he was kneeling in the sand—
a smell of wood burning the air,
his fingertips digging like moles
trying to touch
just one notched stone.

DART AND I TRY VOODOO

We genuflect on the wrong knee.
In the tarpaper garage loft,
we shake Pillsbury Flour
above my sister's stuffed doll. Small clouds
explode, disappear
in air like ghosts' laughs.
Chants sizzle from our wooden lips.

We don't think of the nuns nodding,
Hail Marys marching from our throats.
This is the other side of prayer.

We stick the pin
into the doll, see little Amy stumble
on the driveway. We grin at
the red meteor flying down her shin.

Stick the pin again. In a few minutes
the wheel of Mark's bicycle
has its teeth knocked out by a tree.

Dart and I stare at each other,
our eyes shiny buttons.
Our skin is suddenly pale
and dry like cloth, the way it felt
after we burned lighter fluid
in our cupped hands.

Outside, the hot summer air is too close.
It slides into our bodies,
a deep pin.

SATURDAY AFTERNOON,
CY WENDT SEARCHES FOR THE FIRE

Cy will not leave his yard.
He stretches for a glimpse, head wobbling
like a rusted oil can balanced on a
fencepost. Above the trees, smoke rises black
as Monday's headlines, smudged as his past:
> He remembers the first time his head began to
> twitch, like a man forever saying no.
> The way the railroad steam in his blood
> suddenly condensed into plain water.
> Then, with the tilt in his neck, the whole world
> tipped sideways,
> the disease he never understood.

He wonders if it could be Kluge's Gas Station
or Kuwitsky's shed.
Kids with bikes slice
his yard in two, half
the town runs in the street toward the shouting smoke.

> At work Cy always keeps the same speed
> on his tram car, listens to greased wooden ties
> passing, metronome beats.
> The switch signs hold up their paint-chipped crosses.
> Each day he bends on one knee, head
> jerking, to check the line
> of the rail. He can never quite see
> if it's straight.
> Everyone knew he'd stay for good
> the day he left coins on the tracks.

Water from firehoses carves colorless rainbows in the air,
and Cy shakes and wonders.
> wonders and shakes.

Something beneath Cy's skin burns—
it's that same pain. Like pennies
flattened hot on shiny tracks.

15

He waits for sleep, for layers
of sooty air to lie down on his sheets.
He tries not to think of the future,
the thousand days of earthquakes, of fires,
the small disasters
no crowds will flock to see.

HONEY LADY

She takes off all her clothes,
walks to the cupboard
filled with bottles of honey. She pours
the liquid over her pale body,
smiles as if she just slid into
the most expensive, elegant dress,

and she is ready. She opens
the back door, steps
into her secluded yard.
Thick honey magnifies
the heat of the September sun.

Her wrinkles think they hear
a dog whimper somewhere, a teenage boy's nostrils
fogging a circle on an upstairs window,
a man across the river, the lenses
of his binoculars whining.

She strolls and folds her hands,
praying there will be no rain today
to wash her clothes from her, wash
away her golden skin, leave
a yellow stain in the grass where ants
would drown, leave her
naked as an empty jar.

She will stay outside all afternoon
while the shifting winds
lift the first dry leaves
that kiss her and stick
to every sweet part.

THE SLAUGHTERHOUSE BOYS

Abandoned. My brother and I tiptoed
in. A cement floor
where pink stains
stuck flat fingers
into a drain.
Everywhere: hooks, rusted chains,
iron pinchers the color
of the liverwurst sky.
Our bare kneecaps felt the tips of butcher knives.

What did they once kill here?
Why did this bruised door keep its mouth
open for us? We remembered cutting
our arms on broken bottles,
part of our childhood dripping out.

In bed that night we both heard the moans
of ghost cows or pigs or
whatever died and died there
at midnight with no one looking.

Each night after that we were middle aged, fat,
wore white aprons with stained hearts showing.
Each night we slapped the silver cleavers
against our own wrists.
Each night, in that cement silence,
we were the only witnesses.

THE FIRST THAW:
PLANTING IN THE BACK YARD

My father and I planted today.
Stalked out, back of the house,
spiders on water. He hunted
for some time, saying
roots will not bother us.

He found the perfect place,
listened to the worms singing.

We stabbed the taut ribbons
of grass quickly
boxes of sod,

shovels did not pause for
breath slicing rocks
like raw potatoes

we finally
stopped. Not even sweating,
jumped in.

Began filling in the hole
around us.

THE WIDOW WOMAN WHO HEARS THE BATS

But why do they keep scratching inside the walls
like that? Don't they ever sleep?

They keep her up all night, making their sound
like insects trying to crawl their way
out of a dead man's belly. She turns
all the lights on. She thinks of making breakfast,
but it's just barely midnight. She squeezes a soup spoon
in each hand, while the bags under her eyes
expand, black balloons.

She is too afraid to imagine their charcoal bodies,
their red mouths breaking the skin of plaster
and opening, speechless wounds.

She pulls down all the shades. She leaves
the refrigerator door open
and stares long minutes at the porcelain,
falling in love with its brightness.

If she does sleep, she thinks she sleeps
with her eyes open, skittering nervous as moths.
And when she wakes she never tries to remember her dreams
of riding on rubbery wings
that must take her to a cave
dark as a coffee pot full of fear.

THE WATER TOWER CLIMBERS

Their home town's name looms just
above them, more massive
than any thunderhead they've ever imagined.
They don't know those letters
will weigh down their shoulders
the rest of their lives—
they're strong, they're 16, they squeeze
cans of beer. They're in love with heights,
want to see all the tavern lights shrink
to blinking jewels, all those streets
become arrows of dust aimed at the limits.

Three steps from
the top, the wind
tries to blow
the first whiskers
from their faces.

At last they let go
the railing, and
balance, thinking
we could fit this whole town on our thumbnails.

WINTERING IN AMERICA

1

The women bow and pray over movie magazines
in the laundromat. They can feel me
walking across the back pages of their sight
but do not turn to look.

Outside, I wonder why these storefronts
are flat, unshuffled cards,
each with its own blank face.

2

I have remembered smells.
My nostrils have been amazed
by smoked meats at the market:
in midwinter, they have carried me
almost all the way to July.
      "Fishing? Rent your boat from Angorski,
      find yourself on Great Loon Lake."

I have heard the antique clocks
clearing their brass throats at old Emily's.
She uses the Chlorox bottle
to keep the door of her flat closed at night.

I have lost myself in the aisles of denim
while the glowing tin ceiling lights
try to melt all the snow
on the General Store roof.

3

In the next town I park my car on ice.
On the square, no one notices
the courthouse clock has fallen asleep.
I am wondering
what I can do to save this country
except walk up and down Main Street, my legs

swinging like pendulums.
Opening the car door, I feel
the scars on both thumbs throb.

4

Some of the men once worked the mines,
others dug ditches before the first snowfall.
Now, beneath the Rexall sign,
they talk of burning down
the ice-fishing shacks.

Small towns are ghosts' hearts.
No stethoscopes can hear the valves
opening or closing, the blood flowing
like rivers to nowhere.

Though I try to imagine honey
small towns leave a cardboard taste in my mouth.

Living here is waiting for a century of snow
to melt,
the earth to heal
its open wounds.

SEVEN A. M. SNOWLOT

I turn the wheel as far as I can.
Feel the car beneath me
begin to skid sideways
smoothly as a muscle moving a large limb.

From a distance my headlights must look
like the eyes of a lost animal
that runs concentrically, without bob or gallop,
eyes aglow with pre-dawn joy and terror.

What amazes me is the absolute silence
of this spinning, as if there were no aching tires
underneath, as if I was riding on something
soft as a dream horse, easy
as stirring my finger in milk.

If I have straightened the car,
I have done it without knowing why, pulled
my gripped fists back
as though trying to break
through locked glass.
So I lunge into the skid again.
I swing, then straighten, swing and
straighten, I am a pendulum, people
could keep time by me.

I begin to think there is nothing left in the world
but this car,
this steering wheel,
this snowstorm.

All the windows are fogged,
but I imagine the parking lot surrounded
by wild animals, seeping curiously out
from the trees, noses flinching at first,
wondering what this strange machine could be.

Now I sense them racing alongside the car
just beyond my frosted sight.
We are carving words in the whiteness,
a language we all understand.

THE FISHERMAN'S LAST CAST

You wake in a small wooden boat as
the skin of your fingertip unravels
into the water,
thin pink fishline.

You watch your knuckles, the back
of your hand, wrist unreeling painlessly
until your whole arm
becomes a strange creature of muscle and bone.

You do not scream, even whisper toward shore
where a line of fishermen stand faceless,
holding casting rods,
tapered candles.
Instead you lie back, hypnotized
by the way the cloudless sky
rotates, an empty spool.

Finally the last thread of skin slips off
the tip of your
toe. You do not mind the wind
that mouths your bare tissue—
the kiss of a close relative.

Look over the edge,
see your reflection
the way you always wanted to be,
free of the heavy landscape of skin
that held you like an anchor.
You are more beautiful than you ever imagined.
You want to grin, or think of flying.

You watch your flesh disappearing
into the bottomless blue lake:
a kite string
released by a child
whose smile is lighter than air.

TWO. TEACHING THE LAME WORMS TO FLY

RETURNING WHAT IS RIGHTFULLY THEIRS

If you look closely at your childhood insect collection
you begin to believe that houseflies are emeralds,
that their backs become green rooms.
If you decide to step inside one room,
you might notice the faint humming, the pins
that hold up the ceiling like silver pillars.

Open the door to the closet.
It is filled with small wings
that someone has plucked.
You must teach each of them how to fly.

DEATH OF THE TRACK STAR

It all happens in a moment, telephone-still.
He leans backward across 30 years in his padded
swivel chair, back toward his high school track.

> A magnet pulls at him again
> from the finish line, the metal
> of his legs is bending, churning.
> He feels the choirs of wheezing,
> a chestful of cinders.
> This is real running he thinks, his heart
> beating hard in his heels.
>
> No one can touch him, yet he touches
> everyone: the crowd arches
> as he breaks string after string
> with his toughened throat and

For an instant he almost believes
he has lived the best possible life—
success pours across the desk in front of him, visible
as spilled coffee. It is the stain
of winning.

He feels a broken glass trophy putting itself
back together again
inside his body. And applause,
like a balloon of light,
surrounds each muscle.

Now his legs can soften into two blue silk ribbons
rippling in the breeze.

> he smiles, and suddenly inhales
> all the breaths
> he has ever exhaled in his life.

THE MAN WHO SUCKED POSTCARDS

Wishing here, wishing there. Blue sky
melts on his tongue.
Every day he sits for hours staring at
the mail slot, listening to the sound it makes
as it tarnishes. He begins
to lose weight.

One morning he notices a doctor in his house
saying "a man cannot live by
one ounce of pulp alone."
"I'm not sick," he answers quietly,
"It's just that all my friends are in distant countries,
licking stamps."

At 12:06 a postcard clicks through the slot—
he hunches, slurps, a gulp, he swallows
but does not smile—it was not particularly filling,
it was only an uncrowded beach
somewhere in Italy.

He vows he will change his life:
for dessert, he buys a 147-page
travel magazine. He begins eating it
country by country.

THE LAST STORY OF THE SIGHTLESS MAN'S HANDS

Can they be that old already?
They never were too far from me, there
at the ends of my arms, always warm, always gnawing.

They have smelled the brown muscles
of a tree's bark, they have tasted
oceans for me. They have listened to
the pores of your face open and close.

And they have groped across the texture
of my own face, with its knobs pushing out here,
its empty places there. Through them I have learned
the landscape of who I am.

And now their skin has thickened
with years. They press
against your eyelids once more;
all they hope for is a touch of snow at the edge
of the ice. Yes, my ten children. My
fingers are going blind.

THE LINES IN THE ROAD ARE GUESSES

You won't admit you're tired of traveling,
afraid to lean too far forward, to push
the frail hinge of your rocking chair
into motion.

You say it would be easy enough to launch
your feet on the dirt road again,
to pry at the nails in your crated bicycle,
expose fresh red paint to salted wind.
This burlap cloth that you wrap around your body
is Mexico.
It would be easy to unwind it.

Once you noticed wooden figures at the top of the adobe church.
You stood and stared as if waiting
for the sharp shadow of the steeple
to carve saints in the flesh of your face.

The more you ride the more often you see
the countryside inside yourself:
     thatched leaking roofs, starving hillsides,
     ribs of broken fences showing. It is a landscape
     painted by a lame brush.
     If a flag waves there, it waves
     beneath a field, opening its fist
     into black soil, testing its way
     toward daylight that lies blind
     as a flattened snake on the horizon.

You learn that your wandering
is a kind of closed cut that never mended,
each step a grain of salt in your blood.

You will move whenever you want, you tell me.
But you stay wrapped tightly,
your lips smothering with the skin of words
you always intended to mention,
names of countries you always meant to speak,
to travel to.

THE PHANTOM OF THE SUPERMARKET

> . . . the cases included in this book will be only of that eerie variety in which the unfortunate individuals vanished totally and inexplicably without a trace and were never seen again . . . men, women, and children . . . taken off the face of the earth by some force ostensibly beyond the ken of contemporary science.
> —Brad Steiger, *Strange Disappearances*

One woman witness
sees me turning
the corner at Health and Beauty Aids, disappearing
like a cloud of Secret Deodorant
swallowed by the wind from the air conditioner.

For months I wander the fluorescent aisles
of the Piggly Wiggly,
searching for a passage
back into the checkout lane.

Eventually I learn
to enjoy myself, sleeping as late as I want
on a mattress of miniature marshmallows,
diving head-first
into the grapefruit for a sour swim,
eyeing young housewives stretching for the diet shelf,
fondling tomatoes and peaches and melons,
leaving no bruises.

On Saturday mornings I stroll
right through the wildest of shoppers,
absorbing all the vitamins from their stacks of angel food cake.
I glide, forever tasting
yet not tasting,
this grocery cart of my life
never more than half full.

THREE TRANSLATIONS FROM AN OLD
FARMER'S PHOTOGRAPH

1

The farmer no longer wonders
how much morning could stream
into his pupils. Or about his mouth,
a stone well that has swallowed
for the last time.

His stare was frozen as it bounced
along the hill toward the windmill.
Now his eyes are hollow, they
listen for a hush
of dry wind scratching across a paper sky.

2

Fog swarms down the hill,
an army of pale flies.

The farmer's yellow straw hat
holds tight to his last thoughts:
the bones of a sparrow in the grass.

3

I press on the print,
feel the stiffness of the light
around the farmer. Something
was about to happen here,
but now not even the grass will
blink its lashes.

In the left corner, the windmill on the hill
watches the highway bloat with cars.
It wraps itself with fog
and tries to hide, like the skeleton
of a man who died standing up.

SALVAGE

I thought my body had stopped, but I hear
breath filling my mouth again with its air hose.
My lungs are flabby tires that billow, then sag,
my worn tongue floats on oil.

I would turn another corner, turn corner after
corner until my body turns
square.

Just look at me, my junkyard: metal teeth
that sharpen with rust behind the
dent of my mouth, headlights that hide beneath
the clay cliff of my forehead,
the cliff where I watch used thoughts
driving off one by one
like old cars.

THE COAL MINE DISASTER'S LAST
TRAPPED MAN CONTEMPLATES SALVATION

Over and over again he remembers that huge black sound.
Some of the men were caught,
their mouths wide as caves, others
stopped in the act of running.

When he woke alone, in a 6 by 6 foot tomb,
he faced upward
where the sky should be.

For a few hours, or days, he dug with his nails
while the lamp on his forehead burned,
one weak yellow eye. Once he thought
he heard their shovels hushing in the coal,
their white prayers far above him.

Now nothing but the constant wheeze
of darkness.
Even while he lies down and sleeps,
his hands dream of digging, eyeballs
still flicker under their lids,
trying hard to remember
the color of light.

DEATH OF THE VAMPIRE

Dusk always comes too late.

The blood around the rims of his retinas
seeths. It sees women's pale flesh
that needs tattoos of roses.
His are the lips that hiss
beneath the silence, his is the ring
of smoke on the fourth finger,
the curious smile
no one can resist.
His cloak becomes
the night sky wrapping
around the face of a woman
until she loves him.

He gets used to the pain of sunrise,
the way his prowling legs
start to limp
as if all their arteries
were pumping plain air,
the terror of being an ordinary man
sleeping too long in a dark suit.

He dreams of his veins stretching
halfway around the world
as he feels the wood in his heart
beginning to pulse.

AN AIRMAN IN EUROPE, LISTENING FOR ECHOES

Beneath the Dream

You're still over there
sitting somewhere under a shower
or a brothel, making
pictures with the girl in Pomplona.

The rain, pummel of
rain, and you turn your wings
into a long sleep,
to another smell of sweat or love.

You feel the dream again,
soundless as a painting. Is it
the close fire of bulls?

Lunch, Where Ever You Find Her.

Those sandwiches. Strange
meats in them. She held hers
to your mouth too god damned hot you said
the bread isn't bad.

Drawing with her toes
under the table, a cape of dust
rising and hovering.

Evening Wine Across the Sky.

Your letters home were soaked
pink and limp

12 o'clock high
you exploded every day—
wine-lipped women you memorized.

The night turns to salt
and your fist falls silent;
a thin glass hides in the window.

THE MAGICIAN'S DREAM OF SAFETY

This is the storm you have hoped for:
where we stand, the field darkens.

You say you remember the time
we rested here on a rock—
grass blades pushed away our footprints for a moment
our minds forgot the bones of clocks,
covers that tightened
at the end of each day
                    at 3:00 they will wrap you in rope
                    put you in a large jar
                    lower you into the swirling clouds
                    of the river.
                    You will
                        Return Alive
                        In 3 Minutes
                    your posters said so.

            You've memorized the warm sounds of fingers.

Upon this rock is your heaven
of broken glass

bad luck hides
everywhere you tell me
night might rush into you, a deep breath
of water.

As you turn and walk
away, another dream fills your skull.

The last edge of light I see
you at the corner of the woods,

blood oozing through your shirt pocket
while you cut
the feet off a rabbit.

THE UFO IN IOWA

Yes. He does see it.
This silver egg of light
hatches above the farmer's barn,
already his legs are running toward it,
his tongue rattling speechless and numb
like a stone dropped into a tin bucket.
> He forgets all those years of nights in his field,
> sipping whiskey, poised until 2 or 3,
> poking his one long metallic eye
> above dry cornstalks.
> He often thought of converting the aliens to God,
> of opening a Bible
> in front of their weird, ignorant faces.
Now this saucer steals the last of his gasps as it
lands near the pond.
He waits shivering, ankle-deep
in the spilling milk of its light.
The faint whirring fills his ears with
the next closest thing to silence,
the sound a soybean leaf makes as it wilts.

A door opens where there was no door.
A figure moves
out, cautiously, as if
it were about to step
onto the skin of a dream.
The creature glides toward him, speaking a
buzzing cicada language
he cannot understand.

The farmer sways,
a flannel shirt blowing on a clothesline.
The visitor carries something that looks
like a book.
He holds it to the farmer's glowing, blinking face,
opens it
wide and flat and empty as the middle of Iowa.

ANOTHER DAY IN THE LIFE OF
A LIGHTNING AVOIDER

The sky will always look overcast when you wake.

Though you need one badly, do not take a shower.
Lightning could sneak through the pipes
like murderous water,
show you its naked truth.

Avoid putting on the tinfoil slippers
your mother gave you for Christmas.

Then eat your Instant Breakfast slowly,
with a plastic spoon. While chewing,
try not to daydream about anything metallic.

When you're dressed for work at last,
claw a tunnel under the yard
to the garage.
Return to the house without touching
the door handle of your car.
Hide your keys
in a bowl of hardening Jello.

By afternoon, when massive clouds gather,
put on your rubber wetsuit and take a nap.
            You dream you are at the bottom of a lake;
            you have become a Budweiser beer can.
            Safe from the caving-in of thunder,
            you listen to the slow, happy music
            of your own rusting.

THE WOMAN WHO ATE LIGHT

Each evening she set her alarm to ring just before sunrise.
She was ready to break the first ray of light
in half and eat it,
a long yellow loaf of bread.

But years of waiting through the long blackness
made her anxious,
so one night she twisted the bright light bulb
from the ceiling,
put it into her mouth.
This is not as good as light, she thought,
but it will do until dawn.
She chewed and chewed
on glass and filaments,
savored them
until she tasted sweet juices.

Her friends told her she should live on darkness instead,
because nights last longer than days.
No, she answered, light
has the better flavor.
Some day I will give birth to light, she told them,
some day I will raise a whole house full of it.

They laughed at her, but she is happy
just to lie in her bed at night
and watch the smooth round skin
of her stomach glowing, growing.

MUTINY OF THE ANIMALS

It has taken them all these years.
Millions of horses bent to the callused earth, cows
staring at the weight of hammers raised
above their foreheads.
Thousands of plows, wagons
full of stone and meat. Buried
brains, blind with memories
of fencelessness and green hooves.

Today from the hills behind the farm, a cry
rises up on all fours:
it sharpens itself on eagle's screech and mad wolf's howl.
It rushes into the barnyard, into
every animal's ear.

The farmer jabs his key at a rusty lock.
Animals glance at each other,
moist eye to moist eye.
A chicken lifts its sharp foot
                    over a trembling white egg.

THE ANTIAIRCRAFT HERO

He coughs a red cough.
So he handles the shell gently, a grey baby
about to cry. Once more he pokes his gun at the sky,
where the hum of planes fills clouds
with swarms of bees. Yes,
he will be dead soon, he
knows. His shirt is wet; he glances again
under the bandage: bones
almost showing their pink teeth.

Where to lie down, at
last. Suddenly his legs
turn him around; instinct wraps him in its arms
and he knows where he is going.
None of the men try to stop him.
In a field near the edge
of the village, he finds the quiet fossil
of an airplane, leans
into the smile of the pilot's seat.

DEATH OF THE FISHERMAN

It occurs to you that
the morning light hangs in the air above you
like a halo above a severed fishhead.

It occurs to you that dozens of hooks
might be hidden in your sandwich,
calling with sharpened silver grins,
waiting for the softness of your lips.

You open your mouth,
then close it.
You tell yourself it is only
what every man must do at lunchtime,
reflexes of the nerves.

You are pulled up from the rowboat
and break through into a strange
blue ocean. Your skin suddenly feels
drier than ever before, and too hot.
You pray for oxygen,
but cannot inhale, even gasp.
You begin to smell the slow burn of flesh decaying.
Your eye rotates dully but
you do not see Christ.

ABOUT WHAT IT IS LIKE TO DIE

A crow drums the air around us—
it has fished the sky for days
far from the cities where earth
is a pile of shadows.
In its beak another hair
squirming toward the nest

below, a plant finds itself
in a fissured rock
at midriver

On the farmhouse porch
near the ax with red teeth,
the screen door leans
                away from that winter when the clouds
stopped moving.
                Dad burned the beds and the dog
                to keep from freezing

The crow arrows
toward the sea, a rock
clasped in its beak,
wondering how it feels to drown

We watch the hungry knuckles
of neighbor boys in the yard
waiting for the recaging of the sparrows,
the clacking of necks.

New dust from the field is a black
worm, twisting

                our heads scan the horizon
                for a wild island
                bringing itself home.

47

THE MADMAN'S ESCAPE DURING THE TRIP
TO THE NATIONAL FOREST

they drive us somewhere
in this big metal capsule
the long cement throat swallowing
and swallowing yellow lines
fill up the mirror (I don't pay attention
watch through the windshield at tall trees green candles)
if a door opens I get out

I start toward that blackbird
with a broken wing (I know a blackbird
a piece of night with legs)
keep walking they tell me but I walk
only when the bird limps everything moves
or does not move

I throw bread on the lakewater
it's hungrier than I am (but not as hungry
as the puddle behind my forehead)
the lake feeds the birds
that are hungrier than it is

when I reach down under my foot
my fingers find a soft handful
of what feels good under it
stones I pull them up I will eat them
like tiny loaves of bread (I will eat them each morning
instead of white pills)
drop those they tell me they try to take me
back

this is the way I run waist-deep
in feet

hours go like broken wings and I limp along this shore
I don't think any more about them
(if a door opens

I won't get in) my temples feel smooth
as lakewater, my pockets are fat with
stones a blackbird follows me
when night comes I roll and roll and
roll in my sleep
and am handsome as mud

THE CONTORTIONIST

For him, any position is fine:
his heel resting casually on his shoulder,
bread dough arms twisting together.
He could even compress himself
into a 2 by 2 foot cardboard box,
still have room
to eat shredded wheat from a bowl, people
pointing and laughing above him
as he chews.

He has almost begun to enjoy arching his body
into an exact O, to feel
the breeze, the universe as it blows
through the open porthole of himself.
He knows this is his fate: to be loved,
to be remembered most
for becoming something he is not—
a chair, the entire alphabet, the ripples
on top of water.
Over the years, he has learned to erase
the wince, learned to relax
with his legs wrapped around his neck,
a thick noose.

For a final stunt, bending
backwards, a spatula between his teeth,
he flips pancakes,
listens to the floppy applause.

Alone in the dressing room
he sits naked on the floor.
Somehow he is nearly comfortable
as he wraps his whole body carefully
into a large, pink bow.
Yes, he thinks, this is his gift to himself.

THREE. THE CIRCLE REUNION

THE REUNION: SWIMMING

To save yourself,
think of your body as the straightest line you can imagine.
Amid this sway of circles
make each motion perfect.
Blend your fingers into a fin,
stretch your legs into long bluish highways.

At first you'll climb waves
like endless stairways, gulp
water bitter as history.
Try to think of your body
as something in flight—an arrow.
Soon you'll forget you're swimming at all;
you'll inhale normally
as when you lie sleeping on your side,
puppet strings of dreams tugging at your wrists.

You'll know the shore instantly
by the smooth touch of sand, the weeds
wrapping around your fingers
like lost pet snakes, green rings.

But somehow the land keeps
pulling away from you—
this small lake widens
and widens like a mouth
that has forgotten
how to close.

You begin to believe water
is nothing more than
a thick, heavy air
we humans
must learn how to breathe.

You look again toward shore:
it's the one small tree on the beach,

the bony arm waving,
the flag of a continent
you will always see just ahead of you
but never visit.

JUST PASSED 23, LOOKING FOR 22

All day I have followed a sound.
I heard it near this beach
yesterday, like the song
of a fish inhaling water.

Today it's not as loud.

The clams smile at me, I wish they would tell me
I'm on the right track: the tide
pulled back, crabs caught in drying kelp,
a fish beached and flopping.
Old mouths opening wide.

When I was seven I dreamed
of the ocean, a thousand miles
away: its thunder
caved in around my thin legs, my body.
I was a fish, sucking the brine until I was drunk.
I woke believing it would keep me young forever.

Before dusk pours ink into the water
I look for a bed
near the drum of a breaking wave

the only sound is the sun
beating on the horizon,
a child digging slowly in wet sand.

MESSAGE FROM A FOUND BOTTLE: 1

"Look into this abandoned bottle.
Walk inside. Stop searching for lost
boxes, buzzing corners. Your hollow
leather gloves tug at you until you thud
to your knees and face the river bank
where nothing sails
but a beetle's husk
in the well of a paper cup.

Now follow me, I follow the yellow drum
of the sun. The music you begin to hear
is this fog rising from the river. Dance to it.
Pull your pockets inside
out, they are useless lungs."

MESSAGE FROM A FOUND BOTTLE: 2

"I am the glass eye
that holds your sky up, and I am staring
back at the beginning:

I remember a boy's hinged hand
writing a note on a piece of ghost's skin,
a boy's breath urgent as the waves
two thousand miles downstream at New Orleans,
a boy's fist closing the bottle
tight as the secrets that flow
between jack-knifed slits on blood brothers' wrists,
a boy's arm throwing the bottle high above the Mississippi,
his elbow snapping like a wet carp on hot slate.
Inside the bottle, the scribbled note
exploded against its creases: 'pry me open
before I drown.' "

THE SMELL OF FISH

You turn your back on me cleaning the smelt,
say you can't look at the slit bellies,
the way the blood along their spines has become
tiny blackened trees.
And I want to tell you it doesn't matter,
they don't feel the fingernail scraping
their nerves to shreds.
Water was the last song they knew
and they still believe in it—
it still vibrates softly
through the grey of their swaying tails.

At dinner you can't finish, saying
their taste is too strong.
They are the river water
you have always feared:
rushing outside our window, its opaque flesh
hides the deaths of tin cans,
rusted cars, drowned women
who stuffed dishrags into their mouths
before they leaped in.

The sink is splattered red and purple,
an abstract painting neither of us understands.
Tonight you turn and turn in your sleep,
unable to wake or drown, still smelling
the faint odor of fish I couldn't quite
wash from my fingers.

THE DANCE WE GAVE EACH OTHER

You and I are the last of all houses.
Outside, the urgent knotting of pines.

In this bed you peel the pillow from your head
and mumble, your words asleep.
"Listen," you say, "did you hear
the crickets stop singing?"

There are better days for building, I know
dreams might not be the music—
is it the puzzle of your eyes
that tangle beneath my skin your
taste citrus quick in my mouth?

The song of your hands everywhere
gathering stones and wood
for the fireplace.

WHERE THE SEASON OF CANOES
TAKES US

Paddling this lost compass needle,
I begin to feel a man somewhere inside me
swimming toward the surface
of my body.
You dangle one hand over the side, fingers
cutting a blue seam that lingers.
We have tried to heal
each other's wounds,
those nightmares of swallowing melted lead.

Sometimes the two lakes of our bodies
merge, a symphony of whirlpools.
Or we're snarled
in sharp weeds, deaf
from the silt
swirling inside our ears.

> From the bottom of the lake I swim upward,
> climbing the fragile pillar of light
> that leads to your face. Above,
> you hold your
> breath for years, lungs
> aching, two pale bruises.

I let go my paddle;
the canoe slowly spins,
the silver hand of a clock
searching for true north.
I look down as someone
rising from long sleep
reaches the surface.
He kisses your fingertips
until all their scars erase.

60

THE KICKER'S LAST STEPS

for Jack Driscoll

One point behind, ten seconds left,
I lunge forward

      a halo of gnats around my head.
      I always thought field goal kicking
      should be easy,
      like pushing a word
      from my tongue into the air.
      But the goal posts
      move backward
      ten yards with each step.

      Am I alone on this field—
      only the yard lines like a ladder I've forgotten
      how to climb, the moon's floodlight
      like a stiff graduation gown,
      the empty avenues
      of bleachers?

      When night fog clutches my ankles
      like the pudgy hands of a linebacker,
      I try to think of anything but kicking
      (the river beyond the goal posts,
      the blank scorecards of my parents' faces),
      try not to think that in an instant
      my toe must dive
      deep into leather
      as if it's in love with it.

From the sidelines my approach must look
almost casual, as though I hardly care—
in the silence of this last step
I hear the wings of three ducks above me
flying toward the creaking ice of the river.

EARTH MAN, THE HARVEST

I feel something like sunbeams crawling
under my shirt. I take the shirt off
and ripe tomatoes roll from the skin of my stomach;
potatoes push brown noses
through my ribs, cucumbers. Even the fingers
I had forgotten curl into green beans.
Suddenly a watermelon raises itself up
from the middle of my shoulders,
and I spend my day leaning
against the sharp edge of the horizon,
    emptying my boots of the dirt,
      the seeds that never stop pouring out.

A JOURNEY THIS NIGHT INTO LIGHTNING

I watch Saint Elmo's fire on the oak branches
lighting the back yard,
scarring the sky

The lines on my palm
are the pattern on a skull,
cracked by the rain rushing
in every direction

I knew I'd be moving, pulling up
the moist roots of my toes

       Near the saltwater pond
       I dream of Saint Elmo, his slumped
       beheaded body straining
       to warn me, scratching
       a map in the mud

I stand up, hands
cupped over my eyes

I see a drying pond
the bald man waving a flag of moonlight on the road
       this new geography
saying follow me
I'm your stranger

THE RETURN: THE SONG OF NOT MOVING

A cloud expands as if it were a deep white lung.
A bird with green wings soothes the bruised
whale's belly of the sky.
The last page of night folds on itself.

    But I lie on my back in the grass,
    and like the exact center of a circle, when I spin
    I travel
    nowhere.

If part of me moves, it is only my breaths
that run after each other, ripples chasing themselves
outward from the middle of a calm lake
where no fish has jumped.

DRIFTING, LIKE A CIRCLE

Whenever you find yourself walking, leave something behind
for the rest of them who follow rivers. Leave
the spokes of your handprint in wet mud,
leave the sparrow you ran so long to catch and caress,
leave the sunlight clinging to its feathers, leave
bits of your face: mirrors;
leave drops of your blood:
rubies.

Touch each place where you've been:
touch the crusts of the bread, touch the worn maps
in their centers where they sag with miles.
Do not be afraid when you
feel them breathing.

When you walk away,
leave the skin you've shed
behind, like a wrinkled note in a bottle,
leave something for them to find, for them
to leave behind.

THE DROWNER

By the time I find him downstream,
                    water is nailed deep into his lungs.
This boy drifts beneath the river's skin,
                    his hair lifting off his scalp like last memories
of smoke.

I watch everything he has learned:
                    the way his arms love to dance slowly
in the current,
                    banners embracing a foreign wind.

Even after days of kissing water,
                    I know he is still alive—
he pushes his face through the surface,
                    his heavy eyes rolling backward
into the wet universe of his skull
                    as if he's in a lost dream of
someone drowning, drowning,
                    sinking lower than spilled hooks
or the small cages of dead fish.

I carry him gently to shore,
                    lay him on his back and droplets
the color of blood
                    keep trickling from his forehead
no matter how often I brush it with a dry towel.

I know I must shake him awake and
                    he sits up, spitting water
as if to thank me. He stands
                    now, gaining strength,
and as I lie down I feel my throat filling
                    and filling
with the clearest words I've ever tasted.